WORKBOOK
FOR

Romeo and Juliet

THE GRAPHIC NOVEL

HEINLE
CENGAGE Learning™

Australia • Brazil • Japan • Korea • Mexico • Singapore • Spain • United Kingdom • United States

**Workbook for Romeo and Juliet:
The Graphic Novel**

Publisher: Sherrise Roehr

Editor in Chief: Clive Bryant

Managing Development Editor: John Hicks

Associate Development Editor: Cécile Engeln

Director of U.S. Marketing: Jim McDonough

Director of Global Marketing: Ian Martin

Assistant Marketing Manager: Jide Iruka

Director of Production and Media Content:
 Michael Burggren

Associate Content Project Manager:
 Mark Rzeszutek

Print Buyer: Susan Spencer

Character Designs and Original Artwork:
 Will Volley

Lettering: Jim Campbell

Design and Layout: Jo Wheeler and
 Jenny Pacentino

Compositor: MPS Limited, a Macmillan Company

Cover Designer: Gina Petti, Rotunda Design

ISBN-13: 978-1-111-22012-9

ISBN-10: 1-111-22012-3

Heinle
20 Channel Center Street
Boston, MA 02210
USA

Cengage Learning is a leading provider of customized learning solutions with office locations around the globe, including Singapore, the United Kingdom, Australia, Mexico, Brazil, and Japan. Locate your local office at **www.cengage.com/global**

Cengage Learning products are represented in Canada by Nelson Education, Ltd.

Visit Heinle online at **elt.heinle.com**

Visit our corporate website at **www.cengage.com**

Printed in the United States of America
4 5 6 7 8 9 10 24 23 22 21 20

CONTENTS

Name: _____

Before You Read

Worksheet 1 – Know Your Shakespeare

A. Choose the best answer to each question by circling the letter of the correct answer.

1. William Shakespeare was born in _____.
   a. London   **b.** Gloucester   **c.** Stratford-upon-Avon   **d.** Salisbury

2. His father was _____.
   a. a wealthy nobleman   **b.** a farmer   **c.** very poor   **d.** a tradesman

3. Shakespeare's wife's name was _____.
   a. Mary   **b.** Elizabeth   **c.** Anne   **d.** Helen

4. Shakespeare wrote a total of _____ plays.
   a. 24   **b.** 38   **c.** 42   **d.** 16

5. He had three children, _____.
   a. two boys and a girl   **b.** all girls   **c.** all boys   **d.** two girls and a boy

6. Shakespeare lived in Elizabethan England. This means he lived_____.
   a. when Elizabeth was a popular name
   b. when Elizabeth I was Queen
   c. in the time of Queen Elizabeth II
   d. in an area of England called Elizabeth

Now read about Shakespeare on p. 164 and find out if you were right.

B. Complete the timeline of Shakespeare's life.

Approximate Date	What Happened?
1564	
1582	He married . . .
1583–1585	
1587	
1590–1613	
1593	
1616	
1670	

C. Circle the titles of the plays that were written by Shakespeare

The Tempest	*The White Devil*	*King Lear*	*The Merchant of Venice*
Tamburlaine	*Othello*	*Macbeth*	*A Midsummer Night's Dream*

D. Can you name any other Shakespeare plays? Make a list.

Name: _____

Before You Read

Worksheet 2 – Get to Know *Romeo and Juliet*

A. Read "The History of *Romeo and Juliet*" on pp. 165–166 of the graphic novel. Then, fill in the chart.

Shakespeare's Sources for *Romeo and Juliet*

Title	Author	Type of Work	Year	Language	Protagonists
1. not mentioned	Masuccio	story			
2.					
3.					
4.					
5.					
6.					
7.					
8.					

B. Answer the questions.

1. Is *Romeo and Juliet* the only play that Shakespeare adapted from an existing story? Explain.

   _____

   _____

2. Which version of *Romeo and Juliet* is most similar to Shakespeare's? What changes did Shakespeare make to that version?

   _____

   _____

3. What changes did some seventeenth-century productions make to *Romeo and Juliet*?

   _____

   _____

Name: _____

Before You Read

Worksheet 3 – Prepare to Discuss the Play

A. Shakespeare wrote three different kinds of plays: comedies, tragedies, and histories. Match the definitions below with the kind of play by writing the letter of the correct definition.

1. _____ comedy   **a.** a serious play with a sad ending
2. _____ tragedy   **b.** a play based on the life of an English king
3. _____ history   **c.** a lighthearted play with a happy ending

B. A **play** is organized into acts and scenes. An **act** is one of the main parts into which a play is divided; it can contain several scenes. A **scene** is a series of events that occur in the same place.

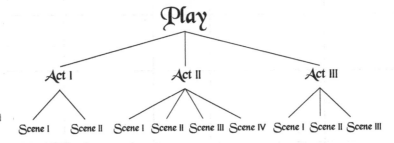

Look at the Contents for *Romeo and Juliet* on p. 3. How many acts does *Romeo and Juliet* have?

_____

C. Match the parts of a play with their definitions by writing the letter of the correct definition.

1. _____ plot   **a.** the words that the characters say
2. _____ prologue   **b.** the story of a play
3. _____ dialogue   **c.** the most exciting part of a play
4. _____ climax   **d.** where a play takes place
5. _____ stage directions   **e.** a speech that introduces a play
6. _____ setting   **f.** instructions for the actors in a play

D. Now match the types of characters with their descriptions.

1. _____ character   **a.** the most important person in a play
2. _____ protagonist   **b.** the evil, bad person in a play
3. _____ chorus   **c.** a person in the play
4. _____ villain   **d.** a person who introduces the story in a play

E. As you read *Romeo and Juliet*, complete the chart below with examples of each term from the play.

protagonist(s)	Romeo and Juliet
prologue	
setting(s)	
climax	
villain	

Before You Read

Worksheet 4 – The Story

A. Circle the correct word or phrase to complete each sentence below.

1. *Romeo and Juliet* is a **play/novel** about two young lovers.
2. Their families are **old friends/enemies** who have had a **feud/friendship** between them for a long time.
3. Romeo and Juliet meet at a party and fall in love **instantly/nine months later**.
4. Their families **want/don't want** them to be together.
5. They have to get married in **public/secret**.
6. Their story ends in **comedy/tragedy**.
7. Romeo and Juliet **die/live happily ever after** at the end of the story.
8. Their families decide to live together in **peace/hate**.

B. Fill in the blanks using words from the word bank.

sorrow	passionate	noblemen	jealous	minstrels
revenge	honorable	cruel	bride	weapon

Then and Now

Italy in the 1400s was very different from today. The country was ruled by kings or princes, and by other 1. _____. Men used swords, not guns, as 2. _____. There were no CDs or MP3 players, so music was always live, performed by 3. _____. Girls were married very young. A 4. _____ could be as young as fourteen years old.

But many things were the same. People were 5. _____ and fell in love. They felt 6. _____ if their love was not faithful. Sometimes they felt great happiness and other times, they felt terrible 7. _____. People could be very kind and do 8. _____ things. But they could also be very 9. _____ and do terrible things, like take 10. _____ on their enemies.

As you read *Romeo and Juliet*, think about how different their times were. But also look for feelings, qualities, and behaviors that you recognize in yourself and in other people today.

Before You Read

Worksheet 5 – Meet the Characters

A. Cut out the faces and then glue or tape them in the correct spaces below.

Romeo

Juliet

Lord Montague

Lady Montague

Lord Capulet

Lady Capulet

Benvolio

Tybalt

Mercutio

Count Paris

Friar Laurence

Nurse

Prince Escalus

Before You Read
Cutouts for Worksheet 5 – Meet the Characters

Cut out the faces. Then glue or tape them in the correct places on Worksheet 5.

Name: _____

A. Listen to the Prologue to Act I as you follow along on pp. 7–8. Fill in the missing information.

CD 1
Track 2

   1. The story is set in the city of _____.

   2. Two rich and powerful families live there:

      the _____ and the _____.

   3. There is an old _____ between the two families.

   4. Romeo and Juliet are supposed to be _____, but they fall in love at first sight.

   5. Their love ends in _____.

   6. However, their deaths bring _____ and end the fight between the two families.

B. Read and listen to Act I, Scene I, pp. 9–26. Answer the questions.

CD 1
Track 3

   1. There is a big swordfight at the beginning of Act I, Scene I. Who starts the fight?

   _____

   _____

   _____

   2. Who stops the fight?

   _____

   _____

   _____

   3. Where and when did Benvolio last see Romeo?

   _____

   _____

   _____

   4. Why is Romeo so unhappy?

   _____

   _____

   _____

C. Circle the word or phrase that completes each sentence.

   1. Biting your thumb is **an insult/a friendly greeting**.

   2. You would bite your thumb at your **friend/enemy**.

   3. Dawn arrives at around **5 A.M./5 P.M.**

   4. A villain is **cruel/kind**.

   5. A wimp is a **coward/brave**.

   6. A feud is a **long quarrel/peaceful time**.

   7. People are usually **miserable/happy** at the end of a tragedy.

   8. Your brother's son is your **uncle/nephew**.

While You Read

Worksheet 7 – Act I, Scenes II and III

CD 1
Track 4

A. Listen to the audio as you read Act I, Scene II, pp. 27–30. Circle the letter of the correct answer.

1. Juliet is _____ years old.
   a. thirteen   **b.** fourteen   **c.** fifteen

2. Lord Capulet says that Count Paris can marry his daughter if _____.
   a. Count Paris gives him money   **b.** Lady Capulet agrees   **c.** Juliet agrees

3. Lord Capulet will have a party _____.
   a. next week   **b.** that evening   **c.** the next night

4. Lord Capulet thinks Count Paris might change his mind if _____.
   a. he meets Juliet   **b.** he thinks about it carefully   **c.** he sees the other girls at the party

5. Lord Capulet's servant asks Romeo for _____.
   a. directions to Count Anselme's home   **b.** help reading the invitation list   **c.** his name

6. Romeo is interested in the party because _____ will be there.
   a. Rosaline   **b.** his friend Mercutio   **c.** Juliet

CD 1
Track 5

B. Read and listen to Act I, Scene III, pp. 31–36. Then complete the summary below using the words in the word bank.

married	Nurse	~~mother~~	madam	wisdom	honor
couple	earthquake	honorable	quiet	married	

Feelings about Marriage

In this scene, Juliet's 1. _____*mother*_____ talks to her about getting 2. _____. Juliet says that this is an 3. _____ she hasn't really thought about. The 4. _____, who calls Lady Capulet "5. _____," remembers when Juliet was a baby. She talks about an 6. _____ that happened when Juliet was only two years old. Lady Capulet tells the Nurse to be 7. _____. Then Lady Capulet tells Juliet about Count Paris. Lady Capulet thinks Count Paris is wonderful and 8. _____. She thinks he and Juliet will make a perfect 9. _____. Juliet says she will try to like him, but she does not look happy about it. It seems like she doubts her mother's 10. _____ about the marriage.

C. Review Act I, Scenes II and III, pp. 27–36. Answer the questions. Include evidence from the graphic novel.

1. How does Lord Capulet feel about Count Paris's proposal.

   _____
   _____
   _____

2. Does Nurse think Juliet should marry Count Paris?

   _____
   _____
   _____

While You Read

Worksheet 8 – Act I, Scenes IV and V

CD 1
Track 6

A. Listen to Act I, Scene IV and read along on pp. 37–41. Then, close your book. Read the sentences below and circle the character who said it.

1. "I'm too sad to dance."	Mercutio	Romeo
2. "Don't be such a stick-in-the-mud!"	Mercutio	Romeo
3. "I know we don't mean to do any harm. But I don't think going to the party is a good idea."	Mercutio	Romeo
4. "You've been visited by Queen Mab, the fairy who makes dreams."	Mercutio	Romeo
5. "Dreams are nonsense because they change faster than the wind."	Mercutio	Romeo
6. "Something's going to happen here tonight—something that may bring my sad life to an end."	Mercutio	Romeo

CD 1
Track 7

B. Listen to Act I, Scene V and read along on pp. 42–51. Replace the underlined phrases with the correct vocabulary words from the box.

formal	nobleman	embrace	masks	holy	ignore

1. _____ Many guests at the party are wearing <u>things on their faces to disguise themselves</u>.

2. _____ Romeo sees a beautiful girl dancing with a <u>man who belongs to a high social class and has a title</u>.

3. _____ Lord Capulet tells Tybalt to <u>pay no attention to</u> Romeo.

4. _____ Romeo would like to <u>put his arms around</u> Juliet.

5. _____ Juliet says that people who are <u>special because they are connected with God</u> use their lips to pray.

6. _____ Juliet thinks Romeo's kiss is <u>very correct and serious, rather than relaxed and friendly</u>.

C. Answer the questions.

1. Describe the Capulets' party.

_____
_____
_____

2. Why does Tybalt become angry? Why does Lord Capulet stop him?

_____
_____
_____

3. When Romeo kisses Juliet, what do they compare the kiss to?

_____
_____
_____

4. What are Romeo's and Juliet's reactions when they discover each other's identity?

_____
_____
_____

While You Read

Worksheet 9 – Act II, Prologue and Scenes I, II, and III

CD 1
Track 8, 9

A. Listen to the Prologue to Act II, and Act II, Scene I as you follow along on pp. 52–54. Answer the questions.

1. Where does Romeo go after the party?

_____

2. Why does he go there?

_____

CD 1
Track 10

B. Read and listen to Act II, Scene II, pp. 54–62. Romeo and Juliet both use **figurative language**. They compare each other, and their love, to other things. Write seven examples of these poetic comparisons in the chart below.

Speaker	Figurative Language
1. Romeo	"What is that light shining through that window? It is the east, and Juliet is the sun."
2.	
3.	
4.	
5.	
6.	
7.	
8.	

CD 1
Track 11

C. Listen to and read Act II, Scene III, pp. 63–66. Match the vocabulary words with their definitions by writing the letter of the correct answer.

1. _____ harm
2. _____ bury
3. _____ heal
4. _____ exchange
5. _____ obsess
6. _____ lecture

a. to keep thinking about something and find it difficult to think about anything else
b. to criticize someone and tell them how you think they should behave
c. to replace something with a different thing
d. to injure or damage someone or something
e. to make an injury or a person healthy and normal again
f. to put something in a hole in the ground and cover it up

Name: _____

CD 1
Track 12

A. Read Act II, Scene IV, pp. 67–74, and listen to the audio. Circle the word or phrase that completes each sentence.

1. The bottom part of a shoe is the <u>soul/sole</u>.

2. If you are polite and show respect for others, you show <u>courtesy/curtsey</u>.

3. An adult female horse is also called a <u>show-off/mare</u>.

4. A <u>limp/lame</u> argument is not a very strong or good one.

5. If you <u>take someone down a peg or two/protest</u>, you are saying or showing that you object to something.

B. Romeo and Mercutio make many jokes in Act II, Scene IV. List two jokes for each character and explain them in the chart. Be sure to include the Act, Scene, and page numbers.

Character	Joke (Act, Scene, p.)	Explanation
Romeo	1. "But tell me this—who were you curtseying to?" Act II, Scene IV, p. 69	
	2.	
Mercutio	1.	
	2.	

CD 1
Track 13

C. Read Act II, Scene V, pp. 75–77, and listen to the audio. Decide whether the following statements are true or false. Circle your answers.

1. The Nurse takes half an hour to return.   True   False

2. The Nurse looks happy and excited when she returns.   True   False

3. The Nurse tells Juliet the news about Romeo immediately.   True   False

4. Juliet is very impatient to hear the news.   True   False

5. Juliet leaves immediately to go to Friar Laurence's church to get married.   True   False

D. Read Act II, Scene VI on pp. 78–79, and listen to the audio. Answer the questions.

CD 1
Track 14

1. What does Friar Laurence warn Romeo about? What does he mean?

_____

_____

_____

2. How do Romeo and Juliet feel when they are finally in the church together?

_____

_____

_____

While You Read

Worksheet 11 – Act III, Scenes I, II, and III

CD 2
Track 2

A. Read Act III, Scene I, pp. 80–90, as you listen to the audio. Put the events in the order that they occur.

1. _____
2. _____
3. _____
4. _____
5. _____
6. _____
7. _____
8. _____

a. Romeo kills Tybalt and runs away.
b. Mercutio challenges Tybalt, and they fight. Romeo tries to stop them.
c. Romeo arrives. Tybalt calls Romeo a villain.
d. Romeo says that he respects the Capulet name and will not fight Tybalt.
e. Tybalt approaches Benvolio and Mercutio. Mercutio asks Tybalt if he wants to start a fight.
f. Tybalt stabs Mercutio under Romeo's arm. Mercutio dies.
g. Prince Escalus banishes Romeo.
h. Benvolio explains what happened to Prince Escalus.

CD 2
Track 3

B. Read Act III, Scene II, pp. 91–96, as you listen to the audio. Answer the questions.

1. What news does the Nurse tell Juliet? Who does Juliet think the Nurse is talking about?
_____
_____

2. How does Juliet react when she hears that Romeo killed Tybalt?
_____
_____

3. What does Juliet tell the Nurse to do?
_____

CD 2
Track 4

C. Read and listen to Act III, Scene III, pp. 97–105. Fill in the blanks with words from the word bank.

executed	grieving	appreciating	sensible	abbey
banishment	sentence	mercy	spirit	ashamed

Juliet and Romeo are both 1. _____ over the 2. _____ that Prince Escalus gave to Romeo: 3. _____ from the city of Verona. Romeo is hiding at the 4. _____ with Friar Laurence. Friar Laurence scolds Romeo for being ungrateful. He tells Romeo that Prince Escalus could have 5. _____ him. But Romeo is miserable because he can't be with Juliet. He doesn't think Prince Escalus showed him any 6. _____.

The Nurse arrives. Friar Laurence and the Nurse think that Romeo is not being 7. _____. Romeo considers killing himself, but Friar Laurence stops him. He tells Romeo that he should be 8. _____ of himself for the way he is acting. He tells Romeo that his body does not hold the 9. _____ of a real man. Instead of 10. _____ that he and Juliet are both alive, Romeo is complaining like a child.

The Nurse gives Juliet's ring to Romeo, and he feels better. Romeo leaves the abbey. He has to see Juliet that night and escape to Mantua before dawn.

Name: _____

While You Read

Worksheet 12 – Act III, Scenes IV and V

CD 2
Track 5

A. Read and listen to Act III, Scene IV, pp. 106–107. Decide if the statements are true or false. Circle your answers.

1. Count Paris is at the Capulets' house.	True	False
2. It is Tuesday night, the day after Tybalt was killed.	True	False
3. Lord Capulet decides that Juliet will marry Count Paris on Wednesday.	True	False
4. They are going to have a big party.	True	False
5. Lord Capulet tells Lady Capulet to go to bed.	True	False

CD 2
Track 6

B. Read Act III, Scene V, pp. 108–118, and listen to the audio. Look for these words. Write each word next to its definition.

meteor	grave	satisfy	inflict	comfort	curse

1. _____: to make someone feel less worried or unhappy
2. _____: to say impolite things about something because you are angry
3. _____: place where a dead person is buried
4. _____: to make someone suffer something harmful
5. _____: to make someone pleased or contented
6. _____: piece of rock or metal from space that burns very brightly

C. Juliet has to hide her true feelings from her mother. Juliet doesn't want to speak badly of Romeo. She speaks with double meanings. Review Act III, Scene V, pp. 108–118. Complete the chart below.

What Juliet says	What Lady Capulet *thinks* Juliet means	What Juliet *really* means
1. "Let me cry for my loss . . . I'll cry over him forever."		
2. "I forgive him, but there isn't another man who upsets me more."		
3. "I want to be near Romeo. I want to inflict the love I had for Tybalt on the body of the man who killed him."		

Name: _____

While You Read

Worviheet 13 – Act IV, Scenes I, II, and III

A. Read Act IV, Scene I, pp. 119–123, and listen to the audio. Answer the questions.

CD 2
Track 7

  1. According to Count Paris, why do he and Juliet need to get married quickly?

_____

_____

  2. What kind of man is Count Paris? Is he proud, arrogant, humble, kind, caring, or selfish? Find evidence in Act IV, Scene I.

_____

_____

  3. What solution does Friar Laurence offer Juliet?

_____

_____

B. Read Act IV, Scene II, pp. 124–125, and listen to the audio. Complete the sentences with a word or phrase.

CD 2
Track 8

  1. Lord Capulet is preparing for _____.

  2. Lord Capulet wants the servant to find _____.

  3. The servant is going to ask the cooks to lick their fingers because _____.

  4. Juliet comes to her father and tells him that she is _____.

  5. Lord Capulet moves the wedding to _____.

  6. Juliet asks the Nurse to help her _____.

C. Read Act IV, Scene III, pp. 126–128, and listen to the audio. Juliet is about to do something dangerous and scary. List four fears that Juliet mentions before she swallows the poison.

CD 2
Track 9

  1. _____
  2. _____
  3. _____
  4. _____

D. In your own words, explain the meaning of the bolded words from Act IV, Scenes I, II, and III, pp. 119–128.

  1. Juliet says she is going to **confession**. What do people think she wants to tell Friar Laurence?

_____

  2. What does Friar Laurence mean when he says Juliet will be **laid to rest** in her family's **tomb**?

_____

  3. Why does Lord Capulet call his daughter **stubborn**?

_____

  4. Who are Juliet's **ancestors**?

_____

  5. What does Juliet mean when she says she will be **surrounded** by ghosts?

_____

Name: _____

While You Read

Worksheet 14 – Act IV, Scenes IV and V

CD 2
Track 10

A. Read Act IV, Scene IV, pp. 129–130, and listen to the audio. Circle the correct words to complete each sentence.

1. When the scene begins, it's three o'clock in the **morning/afternoon**.
2. Lady Capulet sends the Nurse to go get **spices/Juliet**.
3. Lady Capulet says that Lord Capulet **still knows/used to know** how to party all night.
4. Lord Capulet is in a **good/bad** mood.
5. Count Paris arrives with **food/musicians**.

CD 2
Track 11

B. Read Act IV, Scene V, pp. 131–136, and listen to the audio. Write the letter of the correct word next to each definition.

1. _____ a musical entertainer
2. _____ a man who is getting married
3. _____ ceremony that is held when the body of someone who has died is buried
4. _____ to severely harm, damage, spoil something
5. _____ very unhappy
6. _____ the person, place, or thing which you get something from
7. _____ a person who attends a funeral
8. _____ someone who has the right to inherit a person's money, property or a title

    a. groom
    b. source
    c. heir
    d. minstrel
    e. ruin
    f. mourner
    g. miserable
    h. funeral

C. Fill in the missing information about Act IV, Scene V.

1. The _____ finds Juliet dead.
2. Friar Laurence comes in and asks if Juliet is ready to go to _____.
3. Lord Capulet says that now _____ is his son-in-law and heir.
4. Lord Capulet is upset that the wedding celebration has turned into a _____.
5. Friar Laurence tells them to stop screaming and crying because Juliet is now in _____. They should be _____.
6. Peter, the Nurse's _____, asks the _____ to play the song "_____."

While You Read

Worksheet 15 – Act V, Scenes I, II, and III

CD 2
Track 12

A. Read Act V, Scene I, pp. 137–140, and listen to the audio. Read the statements and decide if they are true or false. Circle your answers.

1. Romeo is in Mantua at the beginning of the scene.	True	False
2. Romeo has a good feeling about today.	True	False
3. Balthasar brings Romeo the letter from Friar Laurence.	True	False
4. Balthasar tells Romeo that Juliet is marrying Count Paris.	True	False
5. Romeo visits an apothecary to buy medicine.	True	False
6. Romeo tells the apothecary that the law is on his side.	True	False

CD 2
Track 13

B. Read Act V, Scene II, p. 141, and listen to the audio. Answer the questions.

1. Who visits Friar Laurence on Wednesday evening? _____

2. Why wasn't the visitor able to take the letter to Romeo?

_____

_____

3. Where is the letter now?

_____

_____

4. What does Friar Laurence ask for? _____ What will he do with it?

_____

_____

5. What is his plan for Juliet?

_____

_____

CD 2
Track 14

C. Read and listen to Act V, Scene III, pp. 142–158. Match the words to their definitions.

1. _____ a person who the police or authorities think may be guilty of a crime   **a.** torch

2. _____ an area of land where dead people are buried   **b.** graveyard

3. _____ great sadness   **c.** whistle

4. _____ to make sounds by forcing breath out between your lips or teeth   **d.** insist

5. _____ to say very firmly that something should be done   **e.** lantern

6. _____ a lamp in a metal frame with glass sides   **f.** suspect

7. _____ to repair something   **g.** damage

8. _____ a long stick with a flame at one end, used to provide light   **h.** mend

9. _____ physical harm that is caused to an object   **i.** woe

Name: _____

D. Put the events of Act V, Scene III, pp. 142–158, in order.

1. _____
2. _____
3. _____
4. _____
5. _____
6. _____
7. _____
8. _____
9. _____

a. Juliet wakes up.
b. Romeo drinks poison and dies.
c. The Montagues and the Capulets make peace.
d. Count Paris and his servant arrive at Juliet's tomb.
e. Romeo and his servant arrive at Juliet's tomb.
f. Friar Laurence enters the tomb.
g. Romeo fights Count Paris.
h. Romeo enters Juliet's tomb.
i. Juliet stabs herself with Romeo's knife.

E. Answer the questions.

1. What was Count Paris doing in the graveyard? Why did he fight Romeo?

_____

_____

_____

2. What happened to Lady Montague?

_____

_____

_____

3. Who are the suspects that Prince Escalus questions?

_____

_____

_____

4. What piece of evidence does Balthasar give to Prince Escalus?

_____

_____

_____

5. Does Prince Escalus find anyone guilty?

_____

_____

_____

6. What do Lord Capulet and Lord Montague do to make peace?

_____

_____

_____

After You Read

Worksheet 16 – Matching Quotes

A. Cut out all the cards and match the quote to the character who said it.

"What a good apothecary! It's working so quickly!"	**Nurse**
"Poison! You drank it all and left none for me!"	**Chorus**
"I curse both of your families! Your families have killed me!"	**Romeo**
"All right, I'll go, but the Montagues are going to be sorry!"	**Lady Capulet**
"Every herb and plant is different. Some can heal, and some can do harm. But all of them have a purpose."	**Prince Escalus**
"'Rosemary' and 'Romeo' begin with the same letter, right?"	**Tybalt**

Name: _____

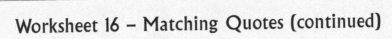
"You'll be in St. Peter's church next Thursday, even if I have to drag you there myself!"	**Count Paris**
"There's trouble in the air. If we meet any Capulets, we'll most likely end up fighting with them. This hot weather makes people angry."	**Mercutio**
"Both your children have been killed. I have also lost two members of my family. We have all been punished!"	**Juliet**
"I wish this foolish girl was dead!"	**Friar Laurence**
"Your face is mine, and you are insulting it."	**Benvolio**
"True love was born tonight. But they have to keep thatlove out of sight. Although they cannot meet during the day, true love always finds a way."	**Lord Capulet**

After You Read

Worksheet 17 – After the Deaths: The Inquest

The events in Verona have shocked Italy. The people are demanding an investigation of the deaths of Romeo and Juliet. Prince Escalus has sent his investigators to question the people involved, or witnesses. The witnesses are:

Lord Capulet

Lady Capulet

Lord Montague

Benvolio

Nurse

Friar Laurence

Balthasar

A. You will either be an investigator or a witness. Write your role below. If you are an investigator, prepare a list of questions to ask the witnesses. If you are a witness, write notes about what you have seen and heard over the past five days.

My role: _____

Notes: _____

_____

_____

_____

_____

_____

_____

_____

_____

_____

_____

B. Now, it is time for the inquest. The team of investigators will question the witnesses. After, the investigators will make judgments about the witnesses. Is anyone guilty for the deaths? If so, what should their punishment be?

After You Read

Worksheet 18 – Characters and Adjectives

A. The boxes contain the names and images of characters from *Romeo and Juliet: The Graphic Novel*. Fill in the boxes with adjectives from the word bank. You can use the adjectives more than once, and you don't need to use them all. Use a dictionary or thesaurus to find more adjectives.

formal	miserable	kind	sensible
honorable	funny	cruel	just
holy	faithful	comforting	romantic
passionate	jealous	vengeful	poetic
noble	angry	wise	helpful
obsessed	aggressive	stubborn	talkative

	Romeo		Juliet
	Friar Laurence		Nurse
	Benvolio		Tybalt
	Mercutio		Prince Escalus

B. Choose one of the characters. Find evidence in the book to support your choices of adjectives. The evidence could be things the character says or does. Write your evidence on a separate sheet of paper.

After You Read

Worksheet 19 – Diary Entries

A. Choose a character. Then choose a scene. Imagine you are the character. Write your thoughts and feelings in a diary entry on a separate sheet of paper.

Romeo

1. Act I, Scene I: Romeo is lovesick about Rosaline.

2. Act II, Scene II: Romeo has just met Juliet on her balcony.

3. Act V, Scene I: Romeo is in Mantua, waiting for news from Friar Laurence. This is before Balthasar arrives.

Benvolio

1. Act I, Scene I: Benvolio has just fought with the Capulets. He has a conversation with Romeo about Rosaline.

2. Act III, Scene I: Mercutio and Tybalt have just been killed. Benvolio has just explained everything to Prince Escalus. And, Romeo has been banished.

3. Act V, Scene III: Benvolio has found out that Romeo has died. And, he discovers that Romeo was married to Juliet.

Juliet

1. Act I, Scene III: Juliet has just been told that Count Paris wants to marry her.

2. Act II, Scene II: Romeo has just met Juliet on her balcony.

3. Act III, Scene V: Lord Capulet has just ordered Juliet to marry Count Paris. This is right before she goes to see Friar Laurence.

Lady Capulet

1. Act III, Scene V: Juliet has refused to marry Count Paris. Lord Capulet has told Juliet that she will not be allowed to live in their house if she doesn't marry Count Paris.

2. Act IV, Scene IV: The night before Juliet's wedding to Count Paris. The Capulets are preparing for the wedding party.

3. Act IV, Scene V: Juliet is found dead on her wedding day.

After You Read

Worksheet 20 – The *Verona Times*

A. Imagine you are a reporter living in Verona. Look at the following news article. On a separate sheet of paper, write a list of other events from the story that would make good news articles.

The Verona Times
LATE MORNING EDITION

SUNDAY, APRIL 17, 1408

Prince threatens rioters with execution
Montagues and Capulets Fighting again

An angry Prince Escalus broke up another fight in Verona's main square this morning between servants and members of the Montague and Capulet families. According to witnesses—merchants and customers at the sunday morning farmer's market—the fight was started by servants of the Capulet family. Soon, Tybalt Capulet and Benvolio Montague joined in. Benvolio denies responsibility.

When asked who started the fight, he said, "The servants. I tried to stop them, but Tybalt came along, looking for trouble."

B. Prepare to write your own news article. Write the answers to the questions below.

1. Which topic are you going to write about?

_____

2. Which characters will you "interview" for your article?

_____

After You Read

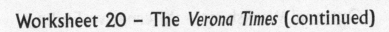

Worksheet 20 – The *Verona Times* (continued)

C. Write your news article on the events and characters in *Romeo and Juliet: The Graphic Novel.* Draw or photocopy a picture to go with your article.

After You Read

Optional Worksheet – Alternative Ending

A. Compare Act V, Scene III, p. 142 in *Romeo and Juliet: The Graphic Novel* to the text below. This is what the script for a play looks like. Draw arrows to label the **setting**, **dialogue**, and **stage directions**?

> Act V, Scence III:
>
> A churchyard containing the Capulet family tomb, Wednesday night.
>
> *ENTER* COUNT PARIS *and his* YOUNG SERVANT, *carrying flowers and a torch.*
>
> COUNT PARIS: Put out your torch. Then lie down behind those trees and listen for anyone coming through the graveyard. Whistle if you hear anything. Give me those flowers. Now, go!
>
> YOUNG SERVANT: This graveyard scares me!
>
> *Exits.*

B. Now, write a different ending to the story. You will write it as a play. Be sure to follow the format of a play script. Use a separate sheet of paper if you run out of space to write below.

_____

_____

_____

_____

_____

_____

_____

_____

_____

_____

_____

_____

_____

_____